Twelve Dozen

LIMERICKS

Freshly-Written Humorous Verse

Philip Wadner

2016

Published by Cade Books

©2016 Philip Wadner

All rights reserved.

ISBN 978-0-9931987-4-8

Philip Wadner has asserted his right under the Copyright, Designs and Patents Act 1988 to be identified as the author of this work.

www.cadebooks.co.uk

Acknowledgements

The motivation to write the limericks in this collection came from author and friend Dr. John Craddock, who sparked the idea of the book. Thanks are due to my wife Christine, who heroically endured being asked over breakfast, lunch, dinner and all the hours in-between what she thought of not only the limericks that made it into the collection, but also the dozens that fell to the ubiquitous red pen. Dr. Craddock kindly volunteered to read through the book before publication, and I thank him for doing that. Finally, I am of the firm opinion that most authors unwittingly include a tiny part of their own life in everything they create, so if anyone I know, present or past, feels an affinity to any of the limericks, thank you also.

Preface

So you want to write a limerick? Think of an occupation, a location or a name and rack your brain to come up with a first line. Then jot down some relevant end rhymes and create a tale by adding the second and fifth lines. Finally, concoct an appropriate event that takes place in between, making sure that the third and fourth lines also rhyme, and there is your limerick.

But is it just a limerick? Although the basic method may be simple to describe, and obeying the obligatory rhyme scheme and rhythm perhaps more of a mathematical exercise than one of creativity, there is hidden treasure. The first line sets the scene, the second a situation or maybe a dilemma, the third and fourth supply the action and the fifth line the denouement. Behold! a complete short story in ten seconds of verse!

Over the centuries, limerick writers have created an unimaginable quantity of these amusing five liners, so originality is impossible to guarantee. However, all of the verse in this book has been freshly written by the author between December 2015 and February 2016, and any similarity to existing works is purely coincidental.

29th February, 2016

There once was a gardener from Leeds
Spent all of the Spring sowing seeds
    He forgot fertiliser
    And was none the wiser
'til all he got back were some weeds.

An old poultry farmer from Stoke
On the face of it quite a bright bloke
    He thought he'd bought pullets
    Turned out to be bullets
And the whole lot exploded in smoke.

A Labrador pup known as Rose
Caught a ball on the end of her nose
    But not only that
    She juggled a cat
Did it all standing on tippy toes.

An optometrist, Paul from Devizes
Sold glasses in all different guises
    Once, a barman by trade
    Asked Paul if he made
Them in litre and half litre sizes.

The forecast one day was for thunder
But the Met Office chap made a blunder
    He had shown the wrong chart
    And it fair broke his heart
When the sun put his forecast asunder.

An Indian elephant called Brett
One day broke out in a sweat
    He asked his mahout
    For some fruit to chill out
And said, Thank you, I'll never forget.

An artist who hailed from the Clyde
Had a goatee which filled him with pride
    He found he could paint
    With little restraint
By using his beard's underside.

A ditzy young girl called Yvette
Got a job in the local laundrette
    She powdered her nose
    While washing the clothes
And bunged up the water outlet.

A rock and roll singer called Mick
When once he was strumming his pick
    With enthusiasm
    His hand went to spasm
And he uttered words non-politic.

A horologist who came from Alltwen
Was correcting the time on Big Ben
    That day blew a gale
    And the hands, like a sail
Spun around so he set them again.

A dentist in training from Leith
Had a client with difficult teeth
    He used a revolver
    To blast out a molar
And most of the jawbone beneath.

And then there was James the optician
Who had made it his lifelong ambition
    To collect old glass eyses
    In various sizes
And start up his own exhibition.

A footballer playing for Wales
Was renowned for telling tall tales
    He said the crowd roared
    Whenever he scored
Resulting in Force 13 gales.

A palmist who came from Holl-and
Could tell everything from someone's hand
    Now this line, she said
    Shows when you'll drop dead
Could you pay me quite quickly, old man.

A wise ice cream vendor called Schaeffer
Was asked if he'd serve up a wafer
    He said, feeling jolly
    First give me the lolly
And then I shall know it's been paid fer.

A woman from Torpenhow Hill
Took up gardening just for the thrill
    But was so disenchanted
    When an onion she planted
Grew into a tall daffodil.

There once lived a butcher in Fleet
Who spent much of his time chopping meat
    Then one day his cleaver
    In a bout of hay fever
Accident-all-y sliced off his feet.

A bullfighter living in Spain
One day took a trip on a train
    After two hours delay
    He shouted Olé
When the train started moving again.

A cyclist rode up Devil's Dyke
But was puffing while pedalling her bike
    Halfway up a hang glider
    Flew close alongside her
Said a voice, Have a lift if you like.

A barber with a shop in St Ives
Had mislaid his hair trimmer guides
    A customer who
    Asked for number two
Ended up with a short back and sides.

It seems that whenever it rains
And water runs off down the drains
    Together with scum
    It must wash away some
Of our archaeological remains.

A colour blind fireman named Keane
Arrived fast at an accident scene
    On his way to the site
    He ran a red light
And explained that he'd thought it was green.

A violinist from Heath and Reach
Played an E and made the string screech
    He rosined his bow
    Still resembled a crow
So was charged with a peace of the breach.

A horror tale writer from Ware
One day lost his talent to scare
    Though far less exciting
    He altered his writing
To a Mills and Boon romance affair.

A fairy from Ashby St. Mary
Once swallowed a dic-tion-ary
    She was soon overheard
    To pronounce her words slurred
And her spells then became arbi-trary.

A milkman from Hebden Bridge
Had a pinta returned like porridge
    Milko said, Wait a minute
    This milk's quite warm, innit
It should have been kept in the fridge.

A builder who hailed from Eastwick
Built a wall but was short of a brick
    Left out a few more
    Turned it into a door
Then closed it and ran away quick.

A fishmonger from Nether Wallop
Had a go at deep frying a scallop
    But it tasted quite funny
    And he made much more money
Selling sauce at a pound for a dollop.

A chap with a first class degree
Had an eagle tattooed on his knee
    When asked Why? without pause
    He said, Oh it's because
My degree's in orni-tho-logy.

A diviner out looking for water
Had decided to train up his daughter
    She picked up quite quick
    How to hold a forked stick
But couldn't make it twitch like it oughta.

A cartographer from Watford Gap
Once had an appalling mishap
    Whilst measuring a lane
    It started to rain
And he smudged half the towns on the map.

An Aussie who came from Gold Coast
Decided to cook a pot roast
    The 'roo that he diced
    Would not have sufficed
So he added some Vegemite on toast.

In London an old apparition
Had ambition to be a musician
> But being a ghoul
> Who'd not gone to school
Completely messed up his audition.

A history master called Fred
Knew the names of all kings who were dead
> Alas, by no means
> Could he recall the queens
In particular those with no head.

A steam roller driver named Pitt
Accepted a wager, to wit
> That with both eyes tight shut
> He could crack a walnut
Leaving all the insides in one bit.

An artist who painted in Louth
Held his brushes secure in his mouth
> He fell on his face
> Brushes vanished sans trace
Until one of them came out down south.

A badminton player named Dolly
Went out in a storm with her brolly
    The wind was so strong
    Blew her over headlong
So she seemed to be playing a volley.

In Reading there once lived a nurse
With a manner surprisingly terse
    Her patients objected
    They some poison injected
Then drove her away in a hearse.

A pet shop proprietor named Molly
Was suffering from deep melancholy
    When an African Grey
    Ordered her a bouquet
With a note that said, Cheer Up! Love Polly x

And then there's a cobbler called Sue
Built a boat in the shape of a shoe
    With a waterproof sole
    It was safe, on the whole
'til the river dissolved all the glue.

A doctor attending the sick
Much preferred to be called simply Dick
    With grave disregard
    One called him Rich-ard
And the doc struck him off double quick.

A post office worker from Stoke
Decided to play a small joke
    He delivered the post
    Disguised as a ghost
In a style that was dagger and cloak.

There once was a vicar from Devon
Preached a sermon on going to Heaven
    A parishioner said
    But you're not even dead
And we need you here 24/7.

One day an investment banker
Was wed to a girl in Sri Lanka
    They sailed off to sea
    Taking gold bars and tea
But the weight in the little boat sank her.

A percussionist banging his drum
Hit his stick on the end of his thumb
    He booted his snare
    Six feet in the air
In an act of pure vandal-is-m.

A genetic experimenter, Will
Grew a species of new daffodil
    Instead of just pretty
    This bloomer was witty
And sang in a falsetto trill.

Then one day an angler named Rod
Took a sharp knife to fillet a cod
    He cut off its head
    But it wasn't quite dead
And it squirmed when he gave it a prod.

A resourceful young woman named Frankie
Was well-known for being quite lanky
    Her feet were as thin
    As a dressmaker's pin
So she bulked out her shoes with a hanky.

A carpenter's mate drank one more
Before screwing a hinge to a door
    He was rather pie-eyed
    And instead of the side
He fitted the door to the floor.

A pair of friends, one of them Murray
Had a bet who could eat the most curry
    One had vindaloo
    The other ate two
And they left in a bit of a hurry.

A woman named Edith from Bicester
Applied to become a barista
    But she spilt coffee grounds
    Over customer's gowns
And the shop gave the job to her sister.

A marathon runner from Pinner
Had never gone home as a winner
    But one day he cheated
    A short cut completed
And even had time for his dinner.

There once was a dancer named Tina
Who yearned to be a ballerina
    She stood on tip toes
    But fell on her nose
For a dancer the worst misdemeanour.

One day a baker called Cyril
Who ran a small shop in The Wirral
    Got fed up with bread
    And started instead
To sell portions of pie à la squirrel.

An antiquities dealer of old
Liked anything made out of gold
    He said, I've a parrot
    That's twenty four carat
In a cage made of gold that's been rolled.

A driver from Rye accidentally
Crashed his old banger into a Bentley
    It was unoccupied
    So he got back inside
And drove away ever so gently.

A heart surgeon who came from Bury
Once suffered a bad coronary
    He chastised himself
    For not checking his health
And for scoffing confect-i-onary.

A curry house owner named Singh
Decided to add in some zing
    So he put lemon grass
    In a chicken madras
And a lime in his curry prawn king.

A crossword compiler called Floss
Was baffled by thirteen across
    She decided to wham
    In a long anagram
Which when solved spelled out Luther van Dross.

In a restaurant, Alan the waiter
Was asked if they served alligator
    He said, For a while
    They'd grilled crocodile
So they might have the 'gator on later.

A cardsharp from Texas named Peter
Was known as a bit of a cheater
    He pulled out a pair
    From under his chair
And was found losing blood by the litre.

An old chap who came from Tralee
Had a terrible pain in his knee
    He felt discontented
    Whenever he bent it
At angles of greater degree.

An accountant from Kempston named Dot
Found herself in a bit of a spot
    She mixed plus and minus
    So her bottomus linus
Didn't work out more often than not.

A personal trainer from Burley
Had a head of blonde hair that was curly
    Although he had pecs
    Like two wrestler's necks
He wished folks would not call him Shirley.

An auctioneer who liked to travel
One day had forgotten his gavel
     So his Going, Going, Gone
     Didn't end in a bong
And his career began to unravel.

A golfer at hole seventeen
Deliberately paused on the green
     He said, You play through
     As I'm slower than you
Mine's a pint when you get to nineteen.

A wily young sailor called Steve
Was granted compassionate leave
     His mother had died
     Near to the quayside
By coincidence on New Year's Eve.

There was an astronomer from Ealing
Broke his leg and then while it was healing
     He hung twinkly lights
     Of reds blues and whites
And star-watched all over his ceiling.

17

A dietician once worked in Westgate
Where she helped clientele to lose weight
    They shed off the pounds
    But it was all ups and downs
Depending on how much they ate.

A genealogist from Westcliffe-on-Sea
Was researching his past history
    But while reminiscing
    He found people missing
Where they'd gone was a deep mystery.

A pastry cook living in Hitchin
Spent most of her time in the kitchen
    Went on holiday
    But after a day
To get back to her oven was itchin'.

A candlestick maker from Crick
Found that everyone got on his wick
    He decided to cleanse
    His circle of friends
And trimmed them out doubly quick.

From Stevenage, Phil the musician
Needed help from a local physician
    A trumpet he'd blown
    Had dislodged his backbone
And thrown everything out of position.

An idle young fellow named Geoff
Liked to pose as a barbecue chef
    But when steak needed turning
    Because it was burning
He pretended to be rather deaf.

And then a greengrocer from Humber
One day tried to sell a cucumber
    That wasn't quite straight
    And was well underweight
So his clients were little in number.

A fencer who came from Markyate
Was busy erecting a gate
    But he felt quite bereft
    When the gap that he'd left
Was six feet and should have been eight.

A poet from Ashton-on-Lyme
Was useless at making lines rhyme
    His traditional verse
    Was somehow made worse
'Cos the ends of his limericks didn't.

A fingernail stylist called Kyle
Had an accident with a nail file
    It pinged down the breast
    Of a pretty girl's vest
And he rescued it with a huge smile.

A young cocktail waiter named Peter
Was learning to make Margarita
    Got his measurements wrong
    And made it too strong
Had to serve it by parts millilitre.

A rancher who lived on the range
Thought his stallion was acting quite strange
    So with greatest regret
    Swopped it for a Corvette
Arranging a quick part exchange.

A photographer taking a snap
Of a pretty girl having a nap
  Touched her leg accidentally
  (Though ever so gently)
Woke her up and she gave him a slap.

A lighting assistant named Jim
Had turned down his spotlights too dim
  There was not enough light
  To pick out Snow White
They turned in their graves, Brothers Grimm.

A twitcher from Wells called Morag
Spent a week looking out for a shag
  Her eyes went quite blurred
  Watching out for that bird
And she missed it whilst lighting a fag.

A web page creator named Giles
Could design in a great many styles
  To increase his pay
  He sat working all day
And ended up reaping in piles.

Whilst sat outside in a jacuzzi
One said to another, Let's get boozy
    The cauldron of bubbles
    Soothed all of their troubles
'til both them felt rather woozy.

A golfer from Wyboston Lakes
Took a wager and increased the stakes
    Although quite illegal
    He trained up his beagle
To hide balls in a couple of shakes.

A ventriloquist playing gin rummy
Lost the game every time to his dummy
    T'was a terrible strain
    To lose out to no brain
As even his dummy was crummy.

A teacher from Liverpool Station
Gave a lesson in alliteration
    He lectured in Scouse
    To a London schoolhouse
And the meaning was lost in translation.

A builder from Barton-le-Clay
Was building a house when one day
    Noosed his neck round a cable
    Fell down from the gable
And those were the last bricks he'd lay.

An ageing Hell's Angel from Darley
Was out one day riding his Harley
    Got a crick in his back
    Hit a tree with a thwack
And that's how he got his nose gnarly.

A conjuror from Devon named Rick
Had a brilliant idea for a trick
    He would take a cream tea
    Wave his wand and count three
And turn the scone into a chick.

A driving instructor from Dover
Told a pupil he was named Casanova
    Instead of her learning
    To do three point turning
They both rolled around in the clover.

And then a young student from York
Did nothing all day except talk
    He was meeting and greeting
    Unless he was eating
Even then he would point with his fork.

A red faced old chap from Southwater
Regularly enjoyed pints of porter
    Down the Old Piggin Wassail
    Was given grief colossal
For drinking much more than he oughta.

A couple in love from St. Annes
Found they had to change all of their plans
    They discovered the vicar
    Had a liking for liquor
And was too drunk to read out the banns.

An apprentice mechanic named Hannah
Liked to tease when she wielded a spanner
    She could tighten a nut
    With both her eyes shut
Then would wink in a mischievous manner.

And then there was Bill from Jack's Hill
Neighbours thought that perhaps he was ill
    He would kick twist and jerk
    Generally acting berserk
Whilst running around willy-nill.

A fryer who came from West Maddock
Was asked for a medium haddock
    He said, Oh my days
    I've only got plaice
And they're in a pond in the paddock.

Now Susannah from near Inverness
Went out shopping to purchase a dress
    It was red and green check
    And had such a deep neck
Where she wore it is anyone's guess.

A homeless young woman called Jenny
Lived under cardboard in Abergavenny
    She took in a boarder
    Who couldn't afford 'er
Though homes like hers came two a penny.

A helicopter pilot named Pearl
Often wound herself into a whirl
    Then one day the motor
    Stopped turning the rotor
Pearl grasped it and gave it a twirl.

A zumba instructor called Heather
Said, Come on we're in this together
    Danced this way then that
    To burn off the fat
Until they were light as a feather.

A Laramie cowboy named Hud
Was cheating at five card stud
    Played out four of a kind
    But the others weren't blind
So they shot him right there in cold blood.

A retail assistant in Boots
Was asked for some bamboo shoots
    Said, my name is Miranda
    Not Chi Chi the Panda
But we've plenty of food substitutes.

A hospital nurse from Dundee
Had a patient who wanted some tea
    Said, it's nae where aboot
    The teem fer yer cloot
Yee'll have to weet 'til it turns three.

And one day a milkman from Crewe
Whose milk float had built up a queue
    Said, There's no need to panic
    I've got some organic
Will that be just one pint or two?

A veterinary surgeon from Slough
Was called out to a very sick cow
    Stuck his hand up its bottom
    And found something rotten
It stank to high heaven, and how!

A friendly young spirit from Haynes
Was learning to rattle his chains
    He hadn't an inkling
    How to do more than tinkling
To this day they remain soft refrains.

A witch from the city of Wells
One day found she had run out of spells
    Feeling down in the doldrums
    She checked all her cauldrons
And found one with the evilest of smells...

...So that downhearted witch from the city
Took her broomstick along with Black Kitty
    Gave the cauldron a stir
    Added a clump of cat fur
And recited a cackling ditty...

...At first nothing happened, but then
When she went through the ditty again
    Realised the thing missin'
    Was a portion of chicken
So she added the crop of a hen...

...The cauldron nigh on overflowed
The witch stirred in a two headed toad
    Her finger tips tingled
    Black Kitty's bell jingled
And a top up of spells was bestowed.

Jelly babies old Bill loved to eat
He could polish them off in a beat
    Although he'd no teeth
    With his gums underneath
He would suck off their heads and their feet.

A steam engine driver named Puck
Was renowned for not having much luck
    Drove into a tunnel
    And knocked off the funnel
Took a tow truck to get it unstuck.

A Labrador puppy called Shelley
Had two feet that were rather smelly
    The ones at the rear
    Were like out of date beer
Yet the front ones were blackcurrant jelly.

A traffic warden working in Barking
Found a parking space with Noah's Ark in
    You expecting some rain?
    He asked with disdain
Noah answered, I'm just double parking.

A young debutante known as Tess
For her School Prom designed her own dress
    Created a pattern
    Like rings around Saturn
Universally dressed to impress.

A talented dancer named Nate
Decided to learn how to skate
    It became soon apparent
    It takes more than talent
As his many downfalls demonstrate.

A cheap decorator called Mick
Had painted a room really quick
    The customer said
    But I wanted it red
Not pea green and slapped on quite so thick.

A rambler from York, known as Pat
Was out on the moors in her hat
    Then quite impromptu
    A gust of wind blew
And she carried on walking baht 'at.

A farmer from times agricultural
Was beset with the view 'twas unnatural
    To convert meadowland
    With concrete and sand
Then erecting instead buildings structural...

...So when powers that be brought their clout
To force him and his animals out
    Built an electric fence
    At massive expense
And refused a strategic buy-out...

...But the powers that be wielding much weight
 Used a tractor to knock down his gate
    The farmer said, Sonny
    I've spent all my money
But your bullying's beginning to grate...

...So the farmer put out a request
For the town to provide a war chest
    They rallied around
    With each paying a pound
And the powers that be acquiesced.

A lock keeper opened his gates
To let a boat through for his mates
    Accidentally dropped anchor
    Regrettably sank her
And left all the crew in dire straits.

A pilot who came from Berlin
Was particularly partial to gin
    He drank half a bottle
    Dozed off on the throttle
Put his zeppelin in a tail spin.

An ill-fated mechanic called Kristen
Was called on to take out a piston
    In an awkwardish manner
    She picked up a spanner
Which somehow she twisted her wrist on.

Now Sally had baked ginger cake
To share with her friends at tea break
    Used too many spices
    And cut them huge slices
They all had severe belly ache.

A Scottish beekeeper named Bing
When he checked on his hives he would sing
    'Let all bees rejoice'
    At the top of his voice
While the bees danced a quick highland fling.

A fashion designer named Lee
Though greengrocer he wanted to be
    Once made up a dress
    Out of mustard and cress
With gherkins hung down to the knee.

In a garden, Sylvester the gnome
Decided he might like to roam
    He went on a tour
    To the garden next door
But the cat in there chased him back home.

A hospital porter named Bert
Was wearing a tangerine shirt
    A nurse passing by
    Had to cover an eye
Before raising an orange alert.

A poet who lived in the Lakes
For a week woke with awful head aches
　　He'd made himself ill
　　Trying to rhyme daffodil
When a host of them's all that it takes.

A motorist one day was caught speeding
In magistrate's court he was pleading
　　I've Labrador dogs
　　Who eat like wild hogs
I was late and they all needed feeding.

A pig farmer's daughter called Pam
Asked her father to buy her a lamb
　　She said, I'll be blunt
　　I'm fed up with grunt
And sandwiches filled with cooked ham.

A rider one day took his horse
For a round at the local golf course
　　It hoofed up the green
　　Not just one, but eighteen
And showed neigh a bit of remorse.

A preserve producer named Sam
Was boiling up raspberry jam
    His wife she was pleased
    Said would go nice with cheese
And cut off a slice of edam.

A TV presenter of cricket
When his favourite team lost a wicket
    With the microphone on
    And decorum foregone
Shouted, Umpire you cannot have seen it!

Ronnie, a teapot designer
Gave one of his best friends a shiner
    He said, I just slipped
    Didn't mean to inflict
Such an injury on me old china.

An elderly fellow named Vince
Was partial to After Eight Mints
    He loved how they felt
    When they started to melt
And never ate other sorts since.

An angler alone in a boat
Was carefully watching his float
　　He struck when it dipped
　　Reeled it in, found a script
From the fish, a promissory note.

A butcher from Bedford named Stan
Boiled up suet in a very large pan
　　While he was equipping
　　The shop with some dripping
He deep fried some Sausage Diane.

Now one day a Roman sartorial
Was asked for a suit gladiatorial
　　He'd run out of steel
　　So said, How would one feel
If I made it from something arboreal.

And finally...

A writer from out in the sticks
Thought he'd create a few limericks
　　With thoughts grandiose
　　He aimed at a gross
The last one of which here it is!

INDEX OF PLACES, NAMES AND OCCUPATIONS

By the same author:

Thinking in the Cloud
and
Other Poems from Upstairs

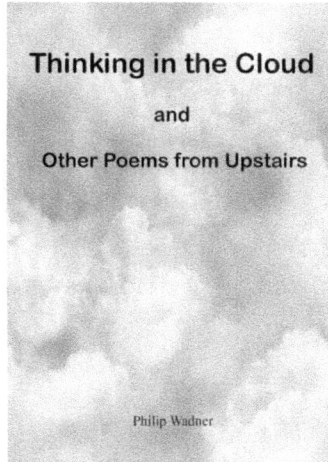

This is a colourful collection of recent poems, which captures universal themes of happiness, despair, love and hope alongside unexpected subjects to surprise and delight. Many follow a traditional form, with examples of pantoum, sonnet, haiku, and villanelle with some comic rhyme, a shaped verse and a rap included for good measure. Subjects range from green cows to charity shops, pork pie to Christmas cake, jazz to wireless sets and to ladies who lunch.

[ISBN 978-0-9931987-2-4]

three cOUrses

Short Stories from Creative Writing Modules

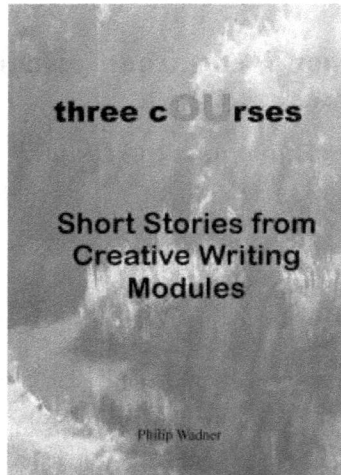

This anthology of short stories brings together some of the author's recent writing, featuring an impressive combination of genres, techniques and styles.

Fifteen stories present the reader with a diverse cocktail of subject matter including hidden undercurrents in human relationships, humour, revenge and heartbreak. For dessert, the author has included ten microfiction stories, each one a complete tale and told in less than 250 words.

This eclectic mix should have something to please most tastes.

[ISBN 978-0-9931987-3-1]

Whomerley Wood Moat, Stevenage

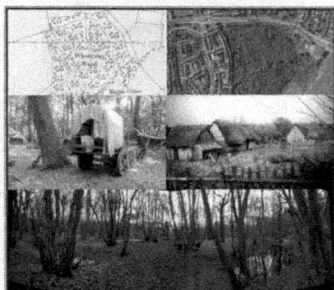

- The House in the Clearing

WHOMERLEY WOOD MOAT
STEVENAGE

THE HOUSE
IN THE CLEARING

Philip Wadner

Believed to have been the home of the de Homeley family in the late thirteenth century, the site of the medieval moated homestead in Whomerley Wood, Stevenage is located about one and a half miles almost due south of the original Saxon settlement around where St. Nicholas Church stands today. Evidence of medieval life has been found there, and excavations on the island have also uncovered relics from Roman times. The author has sifted through a huge variety of sources, and has knitted together facts, suppositions and his personal reflections to create a powerful image of times gone by.
[ISBN 978-0-9931987-0-0]

Probate - A Personal Journey

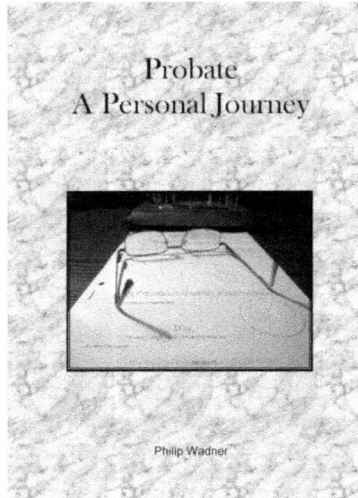

Probate
A Personal Journey

Philip Wadner

After a sad family bereavement, I started out on what I thought could be a lengthy and arduous process of obtaining probate, not least because that is what the legal profession would have us believe. It was not. There were hiccups, of course, but none of any great consequence. The process didn't take long, and it was not expensive. Anyone of reasonable intelligence, who can use a computer, write letters, keep accurate records, and understand official guidance should be perfectly capable of obtaining grant of probate and administering an estate.

This is a diary of what happened to me. It is not a typical 'How To' guide, but is a record of my personal experience. I hope it will encourage others to take the plunge.

[ISBN 978-0-9931987-1-7]

How to order:

All these books are available from good booksellers, or online from Amazon or Lulu.

Or visit www.cadebooks.co.uk for more ways to purchase, including signed copies.

www.ingramcontent.com/pod-product-compliance
Lightning Source LLC
Chambersburg PA
CBHW060624030426
42337CB00018B/3190